BRISBANE

CAPITAL CITIES ACROSS AUSTRALIA

WILLIAM DAY

REDBACK publishing

Redback Publishing
PO Box 357 Frenchs Forest NSW 2086
Australia

www.redbackpublishing.com.au
orders@redbackpublishing.com.au

978-1-925860-47-4

Author: William Day
Editor: Marianne Lindsell
Designer: Redback Publishing

Original illustrations © Redback Publishing 2018
Originated by Redback Publishing

Printed and bound in China by Leo Paper

MIX
Paper from responsible sources
FSC
www.fsc.org
FSC® C020056

Acknowledgements
Abbreviations: l—left, r—right, b—bottom, t—top, c—centre, m—middle

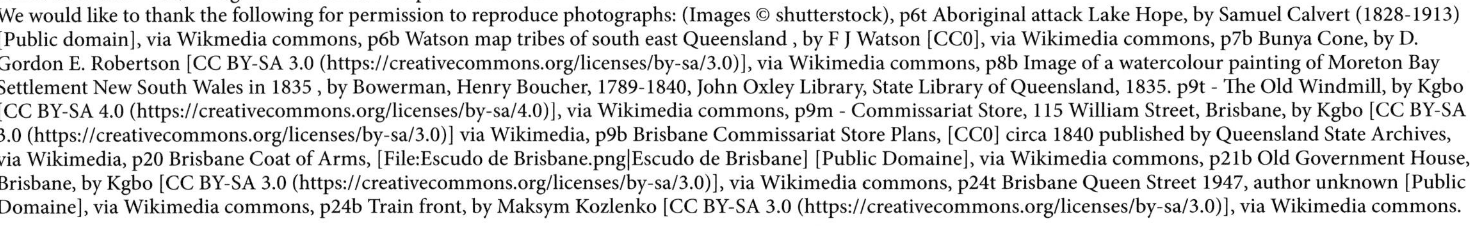

We would like to thank the following for permission to reproduce photographs: (Images © shutterstock), p6t Aboriginal attack Lake Hope, by Samuel Calvert (1828-1913) [Public domain], via Wikmedia commons, p6b Watson map tribes of south east Queensland , by F J Watson [CC0], via Wikimedia commons, p7b Bunya Cone, by D. Gordon E. Robertson [CC BY-SA 3.0 (https://creativecommons.org/licenses/by-sa/3.0)], via Wikimedia commons, p8b Image of a watercolour painting of Moreton Bay Settlement New South Wales in 1835 , by Bowerman, Henry Boucher, 1789-1840, John Oxley Library, State Library of Queensland, 1835. p9t - The Old Windmill, by Kgbo [CC BY-SA 4.0 (https://creativecommons.org/licenses/by-sa/4.0)], via Wikimedia commons, p9m - Commissariat Store, 115 William Street, Brisbane, by Kgbo [CC BY-SA 3.0 (https://creativecommons.org/licenses/by-sa/3.0)] via Wikimedia, p9b Brisbane Commissariat Store Plans, [CC0] circa 1840 published by Queensland State Archives, via Wikimedia, p20 Brisbane Coat of Arms, [File:Escudo de Brisbane.png|Escudo de Brisbane] [Public Domaine], via Wikimedia commons, p21b Old Government House, Brisbane, by Kgbo [CC BY-SA 3.0 (https://creativecommons.org/licenses/by-sa/3.0)], via Wikimedia commons, p24t Brisbane Queen Street 1947, author unknown [Public Domaine], via Wikimedia commons, p24b Train front, by Maksym Kozlenko [CC BY-SA 3.0 (https://creativecommons.org/licenses/by-sa/3.0)], via Wikimedia commons.

A catalogue record for this book is available from the National Library of Australia

CONTENTS

Brisbane Facts and Figures	4
Brisbane's Aboriginal History	6
Colonial History Timeline	8
Effect of Settlement	10
Native Wildlife in Brisbane	12
Brisbane River	13
Moreton Bay	14
Port of Brisbane	15
Brisbane's Beaches	16
Islands Near Brisbane	18
Brisbane and Government	20
Essential Services	22
Brisbane's People	23
Transport in Brisbane	24
Industry in Brisbane	26
Tourism in Brisbane	27
Places to See in Brisbane	28
Sport in Brisbane	30
Glossary	31
Index	32

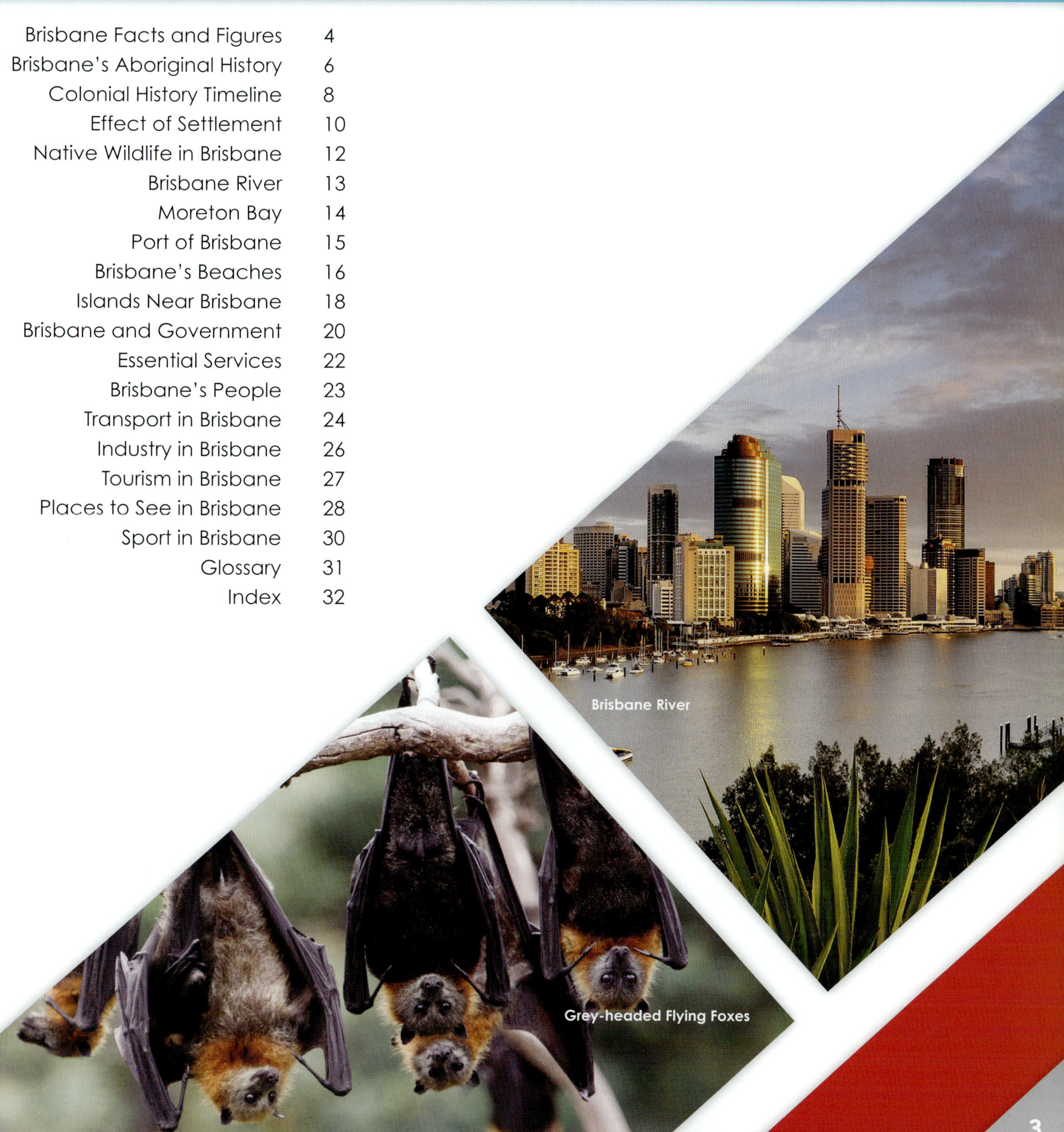

Brisbane River

Grey-headed Flying Foxes

INTRODUCTION

Brisbane is the capital city of the Australian state of Queensland and is the third largest capital in Australia. It is situated on the Brisbane River, which empties into Moreton Bay on Queensland's southeast coast. Brisbane was named after Governor Brisbane.

When people refer to Brisbane they could mean any one of five different areas

1. The city centre
2. The city centre plus its surrounding suburbs
3. The GCCSA
4. The local government area only
5. A personal idea of where they think the city is

Brisbane's Locations

Brisbane includes both a central business district and suburban areas. Altogether they make up Greater Brisbane, with boundaries that include Caboolture to the north, Ipswich to the west, Logan and Beaudesert to the south and the three large islands of North Stradbroke Island, Moreton Island and Bribie Island to the east.

Greater Capital City Statistical Areas (GCCSA)

The Australian Bureau of Statistics (ABS) collects data based on GCCSAs for each capital city around Australia. The GCCSA is not the same as the local government area that bears the name of the city. These GCCSAs can change if the ABS believes a city has grown beyond its previous boundaries. This means that statistics for population, areas and many other things will be different depending on whether the agency compiling them is describing the GCCSA, the local government area or some other definition they have for the extent of the city.

BRISBANE FACTS & FIGURES

Population of Greater Brisbane in 2018 – 2.4 million people

Height above sea level – 0 metres at sea level to about 280 metres at Mt Coot-tha

Area of Greater Brisbane – 16,000 square kilometres

Climate – Brisbane's climate is sub-tropical to temperate

Brisbane's Geology

Brisbane sits on a wide plain crossed by many creeks and rivers. Throughout Greater Brisbane there are the remains of ancient volcanic activity from millions of years ago.

Brisbane's Story Bridge

Moreton Bay

The shoreline of Brisbane was much further east during Ice Ages of the distant past. The whole of Moreton Bay was dry land during some Ice Age eras, and the Brisbane River flowed through it towards the coast, which was once east of Moreton Island.

The large islands in Moreton Bay were formed by wind-blown sand, while some of the smaller islands are a result of coral building activity. Moreton Bay is at the southern limit in Australia where corals are responsible for constructing reefs.

Moreton Island

Kangaroo Point Cliffs

The Kangaroo Point Cliffs, not far from the centre of Brisbane, are composed of volcanic rocks formed over 200 million years ago when lava erupted from deep beneath the Earth and volcanic ash exploded and fell to the ground. The early settlers of Brisbane found that these rocks were perfect for building and set the convicts to work at a quarry at Kangaroo Point. The rocks they cut out were used to construct the Old Windmill and the Commissariat Store in Brisbane. These are now the two oldest convict buildings still standing in Queensland.

BRISBANE'S ABORIGINAL HISTORY

Aboriginal people have been living in the Brisbane area for tens of thousands of years. They were there when the sea levels were lower during the last Ice Age, about 10,000 years ago, resulting in parts of Moreton Bay becoming dry land. The forests, rivers and sea provided abundant and varied sources of food and the people developed cultures that give them a deep and respectful connection with the land and with Moreton Bay.

Early Conflicts

The Aboriginal people of the Brisbane area opposed the new settlements on their land, and the leaders Dundalli and Yilbung became well-known as resistance fighters. In the first few decades after Brisbane was settled, conflict between the local Aboriginal people and farmers in outlying areas was very violent. Some records refer to a declaration of war by the local Aboriginal people.

Meeting Place

Aboriginal people from the central part of the Brisbane area include the Turubul and Yugara language groups, but there are also a great many other languages and dialects with which the local Aboriginal people were familiar. They were multi-lingual and could easily communicate with neighbouring Nations and groups. Early European settlers documented a number of Aboriginal meeting places around the Brisbane area, where people from many different groups would gather to trade and exchange news.

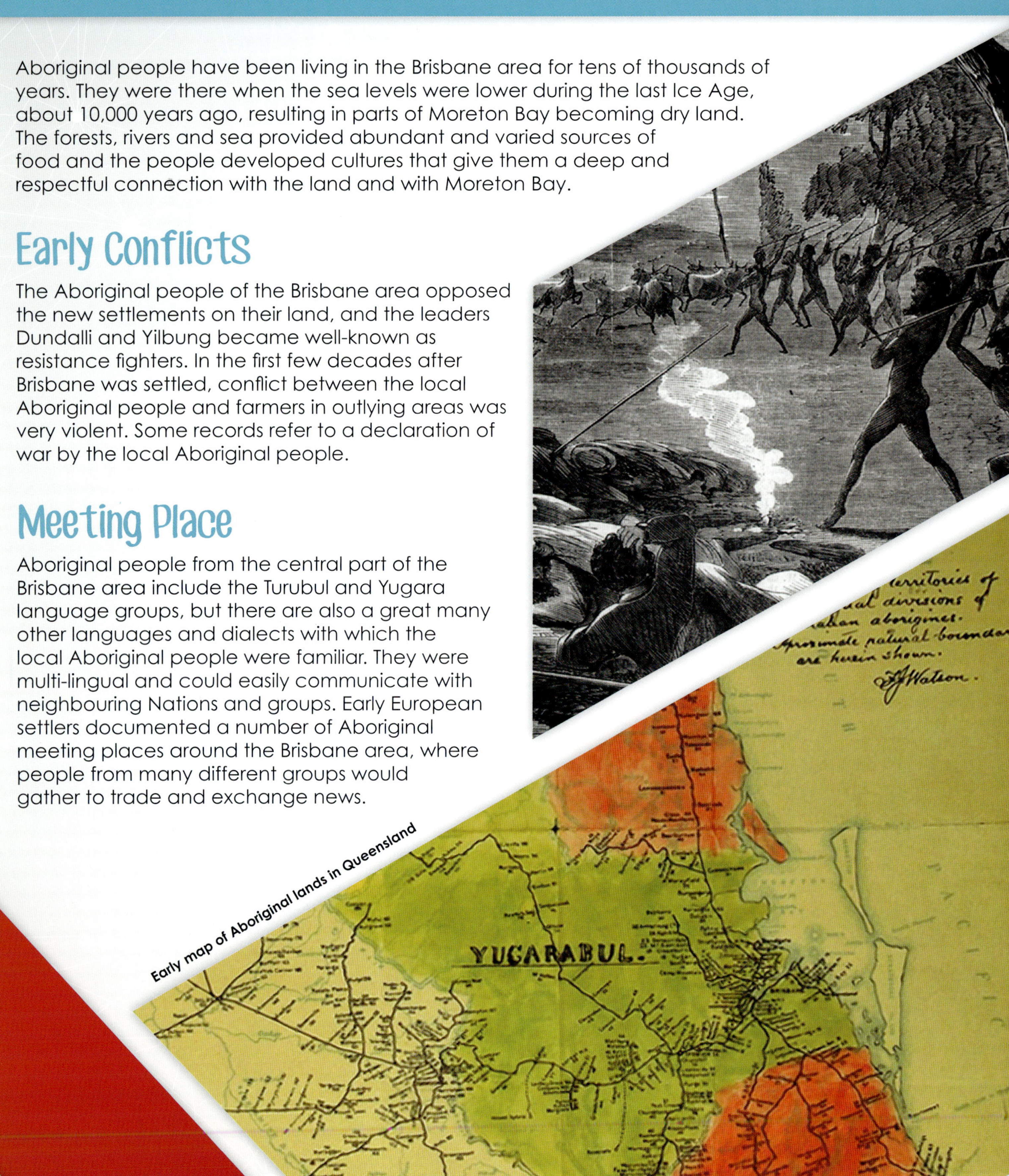

Early map of Aboriginal lands in Queensland

What is Native Title?

Native title refers to the traditional rights of Australian Indigenous people over a parcel of land, based on their customs and law. Native title is recognised by the Federal Court or High Court of Australia, whose role is to confirm that a pre-existing right exists.

Bunya Pines

When the nuts of the local Bunya pine trees were available in abundance, Aboriginal people from far away would come together in the Greater Brisbane area to feast on them. This was such an important event that in 1842 the Governor made it unlawful for any European settler to interfere with the Bunya pine festivals. Unfortunately, the desire to settle more land resulted in this regulation only lasting a short while. Many of the Bunya pine trees planted throughout Queensland were grown from nuts taken from the Brisbane trees by Aboriginal people and planted closer to their own territory further inland.

Native Title

In 2011, the Quandamooka Nation was recognised as having native title over North Stradbroke Island and a number of other island locations, as well as the surrounding water. Archaeological evidence, including shell middens, dates human habitation on Minjerribah, or North Stradbroke Island, to at least 21,000 years ago.

COLONIAL HISTORY TIMELINE

1770
Lieutenant James Cook on the Endeavour was probably the first European to see Moreton Bay as he sailed northwards past it

1788
Governor Arthur Phillip claimed the whole east coast of Australia for Britain

03

1799
Matthew Flinders sailed around Moreton Bay making detailed maps

1823
John Oxley explored the Brisbane River

1824
Convicts and their guards made the first European settlement on the banks of the Brisbane River. It became known as the Moreton Bay Settlement

1843
Free settlers were encouraged to take up land in the Moreton Bay Settlement

1859
Formation of the Municipality of Brisbane, the first local government authority in the state

1859
The Colony of Queensland became independent from New South Wales

1888
First electricity supplied in Brisbane

1902
Brisbane changed from a municipality to a city

Moreton Bay Settlement

Old Windmill

The Moreton Bay Settlement of the 1820s was able to grow its own wheat and maize, but it needed an efficient way to grind them into flour. In the late 1820s, a windmill was built which used large blades to turn a millstone when the wind was blowing. When there was no wind, convicts worked for long hours every day on a treadmill that was like a set of steps. This treadmill turned the millstone which ground grain into flour.

In 1861, the Old Windmill became a telegraph transmitting station and then underwent a series of uses and restorations. The Old Windmill is now one of Brisbane's most important historic places.

Commissariat Store

The early colony at Moreton Bay in the 1820s needed a secure place to use for food storage. In 1828, convicts built a Commissariat Store which had thick walls and sturdy doors to discourage theft. As the settlers became more independent, the food store was no longer necessary. The building then had a number of different uses over time. New immigrants to colonial Brisbane lived there when they had nowhere else to go, and accommodation was also provided for some government officials. In 1913, the addition of a third floor provided more space for government offices.

EFFECT OF SETTLEMENT

At the time of settlement, Brisbane was covered in eucalyptus forests, and Moreton Bay was ringed by mangroves and wetlands. The Aboriginal people who had been living there for millennia had developed a culture which respected the land and its cycles and which did not pollute or deplete the resources they needed to survive.

The new colonists cut down trees to clear land for their buildings. They used some of the timber for construction, fencing and furniture, but also burned large amounts of it. This massive clearing of the forests contributed to flooding as the top soil washed into creeks and rivers, silting them up and forcing flood waters to spread beyond the banks onto the land.

One of the reasons the settlers chose the site for Brisbane was that it had a good supply of fresh water. Right from the beginning, settlers dumped sewage and rubbish into the river, polluting the water they relied upon to survive. This and the increase in population forced the government to seek new water sources further upstream, away from the settlements.

Food from the Water

The Brisbane River and Moreton Bay had been rich sources of seafood for the Aboriginal people and there are records of them trading fish with the first settlers. As the river became polluted near the new town, and muddier because of land clearing upstream, the numbers of fish decreased. The waters of Moreton Bay survived for much longer in a natural condition because of the large area of the bay and the initial small population of European settlers.

Animals of the Forests

Clearing the forests forced native animals to move away from the early settlement. This angered the Aboriginal people, who had always hunted these animals for food and who saw the land being covered in grass to feed sheep and cattle instead.

Grazing Animals

Before European settlement, the continent of Australia had never before experienced intensive grazing by sheep, cattle and horses. The settlers' livestock ate ground cover down to the soil level and their hard feet trampled streams and creeks, disturbing the natural environment.

Feral and Pest Wildlife

Unaware of the massive problems they were creating for people in the future, settlers all around Australia happily released rabbits and foxes, thinking they would be good for hunting. Dogs and cats were highly prized pets in colonial times, but when they escaped into the bush they created the same problems that they do today, killing native animals that had not evolved any behaviour to defend themselves from the unusual new arrivals.

Fox

Cane Toads

Cane toads were introduced in northern Queensland in 1935 to control the cane beetle. They have spread across large parts of Australia and are found in Brisbane. Moreton Island is the only place free of them near Brisbane. Cane toads are poisonous and can kill other animals that may try to eat them. The release of the cane toad is an example of how not to undertake biological control of one pest by another.

Cane Toad

Deer

Deer were released into the bush around Brisbane in the 1800s to provide an animal for the sport of hunting. They are now a pest as they can cause accidents on roads, their hooves damage the ground and they compete with native animals for food.

Rodents

Mice and rats came to Brisbane hidden in cargo on ships. They infested homes, and have multiplied to plague numbers at various times in the past. They established quickly in the early town and have been pests ever since.

Guppies and Carp (Goldfish)

These fish are in Brisbane's waterways as a result of aquarium owners releasing them when they no longer want to keep them as pets. This is a very destructive action as fish such as these can destroy the delicate ecosystems of natural waterways, lakes and ponds.

Garden Plants

Many garden plants that settlers brought to Brisbane have spread into bushland, where they became damaging weeds. In Brisbane, salvinia and water hyacinth are amongst these unwanted plants.

Actions Against Pest Wildlife

Brisbane City Council has a range of measures that attempt to keep invasive plants and animals under control. These include the humane disposal of pest animals and the clearing of weeds from natural areas. Home owners should ensure they are not encouraging pest wildlife by releasing pets into the bush or any waterways, or by growing weed plants in their gardens.

NATIVE WILDLIFE IN BRISBANE

Despite the growth of the city and its suburbs, there are many native plants and animals that live in the Greater Brisbane area.

Grey-headed Flying Foxes

Birds

Magpies, Brush Turkeys, Noisy Miners, Butcherbirds, Crows, Australian White Ibis, Parrots, Honeyeaters, Ducks, Kookaburras and Rainbow Lorikeets.

Mammals

Flying Foxes, Possums, Gliders, Kangaroos and Wallabies.

Rainbow Lorikeet

Under Threat

Koalas and Glossy Black Cockatoos.

Marine Animals

Dugongs, Dolphins, Turtles and Whales.

Dugong

BRISBANE RIVER

The Brisbane River's Aboriginal name is Maiwar. Aboriginal people have long fished its waters and used canoes to travel along its course.

The first European settlers chose the site for Brisbane based on their need for fresh water. The Brisbane River supplied the colony with its drinking water, and with a means of travel before roads were built though the forests.

The Brisbane River is an ancient waterway that once flowed further out to the Coral Sea when the sea levels on Earth were all much lower.

Today, the long Brisbane Riverwalk provides locals with space for exercise and enjoying the riverside views on bicycle or on foot. The first Riverwalk structure was spectacularly destroyed when the 2011 floods washed it away.

Brisbane Flood, 2011

Floods

The Brisbane River has always created havoc when it floods, right from the time when the first settlers of Brisbane were living beside it. Bridges across it were frequently destroyed by raging floodwaters.

In 2011, the worst floods in living memory caused the Brisbane River to inundate suburbs as well as parts of the Brisbane city centre. The flooded river swept away structures along its course and caused an enormous amount of damage.

Brisbane Flood, 2011

MORETON BAY

Moreton Bay's waters flow into the Coral Sea to the east. The bay's shallow waters have seagrass beds and coral reefs, and there are still remnants of the mangrove forests and wetlands that used to line its shores. The wildlife of the bay includes dugongs, dolphins, turtles and whales. There are over 300 islands in Moreton Bay. Some are inhabited, while others have restricted access.

Queenslands National Parks Service recommends these steps to avoid harming dugongs in Moreton Bays Seagrass beds

1. When boating, go slowly over seagrass beds and observe speed limits
2. Use bait-disposal bags
3. Do not dispose of plastic, nets, fishing line or rope in the water

Moreton Bay includes lanes for commercial shipping. Its waters and beaches also attract locals and visitors for recreation, environmental tourism and fishing.

The Moreton Bay Marine Park was created in 1993.

Sea Turtle entangled in a fishing net

Environmental Threats to Moreton Bay

- Creeks and rivers wash pollutants into the bay
- Discarded nets and fishing lines can strangle turtles
- Marine animals can ingest plastic and other litter
- Silt that covers seagrass beds can impact on the food source of local dugongs
- Human population growth can result in competition with wildlife for use of the bay's waters

PORT OF BRISBANE

Brisbane's main shipping port is located on Fisherman Island. During the 1800s, wharves around Moreton Bay were Brisbane's point of contact with international shipping taking timber, coal and agricultural products to the rest of Australia and overseas. Imports to Brisbane from other countries came on sailing and later steam ships across Moreton Bay and docked near the city.

Dredging

Silt flowing into Moreton Bay from rivers and creeks has resulted in dredging being necessary right from the early days of the colony in the 1860s. Moreton Bay is shallow in parts and is dredged to stop heavy shipping becoming stuck in mud on the seabed.

BRISBANE'S BEACHES

Being located on a bay means that Brisbane has beaches in every direction. The islands in Moreton Bay are also renowned for their idyllic beaches, where visitors can escape the city and be on a quiet island after only a short boat ride or drive across a bridge.

Although the surf is not as large as at beaches exposed to the Pacific Ocean, Brisbane's nearby beaches make up for this with their unspoiled surroundings. Because there are so many small beaches, they are not all patrolled by lifeguards, so swimmers need to take care. There are sometimes dangerous swimming conditions.

Cylinder Beach

North Stradbroke Island Beaches

Adder Rock Beach
Amity Point Beach
Cylinder Beach
Deadman's Beach
Flinders Beach
Frenchman's Beach
Home Beach
Main Beach

Moreton Island Beaches

Bulwer Beach
Cowan Beach
Honeymoon Bay
Kooringal Beach
Tangalooma Beach
The Surfside
Yellow Patch Beach

Bribie Island, near the Bongaree jetty

Bribie Island Beaches

Banksia Beach
Bongaree Beach
Red Beach
Skirmish Point
Sylvan Beach
Woorim Beach

Moreton Island

Moreton Bay Beaches

Beachmere
Bongaree Beach
Colmslie Beach
Deception Bay
Godwin Beach
Hays Inlet
Lower Moore Park
Margate Beach
Nudgee Beach
Raby Bay
Sandgate
Suttons Beach

STREETS BEACH

Streets Beach at South Bank in Brisbane is a permanent artificial beach. The lagoon is patrolled by lifeguards and the water provides an alternative to a public swimming pool for inner-city dwellers.

Streets Beach in South Bank Parkland

ISLANDS NEAR BRISBANE

Moreton Bay has hundreds of islands administered by various local and state government agencies.

North Stradbroke Island

With an ancient history of Aboriginal occupation, North Stradbroke Island, or Minjerribah, is one of the most interesting places to visit in Moreton Bay. It is the second largest sand island in the world, and its separation from South Stradbroke Island occurred in the 1890s following a storm which blew away the sand joining them together. The island housed a quarantine station in the mid-1800s and later, during the Second World War, coastal defence operations there helped keep Brisbane secure from enemy attacks. Today, visitors to North Stradbroke Island can enjoy its forests, wetlands, beaches and shore-based whale-watching.

Bribie Island

Bribie Island is a tourist attraction with beautiful beaches and forests. A bridge connects it to the mainland, allowing tourists to take their 4WD vehicles to explore the nature trails and beaches.

Moreton Island

Moreton Island is the third largest sand island in the world. Its lakes, beaches, sand dunes and wildlife make it a perfect destination for a short stay near Brisbane. Wild dolphins delight tourists by swimming up to them to be hand-fed, and snorkelers can explore the wrecks that form a purpose-made breakwater. The lighthouse at Cape Moreton on the island was the first in Brisbane.

Defensive bunkers built on Moreton Island during the Second World War were designed to protect Brisbane from enemy attack.

North Stradbroke Island

Bribie Island

Green Island

Green Island is a small coral island which was once mined to make the lime used in cement. It is one of the most southerly coral reef islands in Australia.

Bulwer Island

Bulwer Island is an artificially raised island near where the Brisbane River enters Moreton Bay. It was the site of a lighthouse until 1983, and an oil refinery which closed in 2015.

Mud Island

Despite its unpleasant name, Mud Island is a wildlife haven and covered in mangroves.

Fisherman Island

The Port of Brisbane is located on Fisherman Island at the mouth of the Brisbane River. It is connected to the mainland by a bridge along Port Drive. The port facility is on reclaimed land formed when smaller islands were joined together.

St Helena Island

The isolated ruins of a convict prison make St Helena Island a place of interest for people who want to find out about the history of Brisbane.

St Helena Island National Park

BRISBANE AND GOVERNMENT

Brisbane City Council

Brisbane City Council is the local government body responsible for the city centre of Brisbane and a large part of Greater Brisbane. It dates from 1859 and its first mayor was John Petrie. The area it covers has the biggest population of any local government jurisdiction in Australia. In 1924, the city area increased when a number of small municipalities and the existing Brisbane council all joined together. Today, Brisbane City Council has189 suburbs, plus locations on islands in Moreton Bay.

King George Square

Opened in 1975, King George Square is in front of City Hall. The statues in the square all have important connections to Brisbane and its history.

- Petrie Tableau – Members of the Petrie family were early settlers in Brisbane
- King George V Memorial – Honours the monarch at the time City Hall opened
- Speakers' Corner with statues of:
  - Steele Rudd, an author
  - Emma Miller, a suffragette
  - Sir Charles Lilley, a former Premier of Queensland

Brisbane City Hall

Brisbane City Hall dates from 1930, when it was considered one of the most magnificent buildings in all of Australia. The clock tower rises over 90 metres from ground level and for many years was the tallest structure in the state.

Brisbane Coat of Arms

- The shield of the Coat of Arms is supported by two gryphons. A gryphon is a legendary creature representing authority and protection
- Blue and gold are the city's official colours
- The motto is 'We Aim For the Best'

Emblems of Brisbane

Floral Emblem

Red Poinsettia

Animal Emblem

Tree Frog

Brisbane's Flag

The symbols on the flag are based on those of the Coat of Arms

QUEENSLAND'S STATE PARLIAMENT

Brisbane is the location of Queensland's State Parliament. Parliament House in Brisbane is unusual amongst Australia's state parliament buildings as it needs only one house of assembly for its elected members. Queensland has a unicameral system of state government, meaning that it has only one house, the Legislative Assembly. The second House, the Legislative Council, was abolished in 1922.

Parliament House

The first Parliament House was located in the Convict Barracks in Queen Street, Brisbane from 1860. Prior to this, the barracks had been used for various government purposes. This old building no longer exists.

Work on the new Parliament House began in 1864 and finished twenty five years later in 1889. Its cost ran way over budget and there were many delays due to the effects of economic depression in the 1860s, as well as problems sourcing building materials.

Old Government House

When Queensland became a separate colony in 1859, it also gained its own Governor. The architect Charles Tiffin designed a government house building which was a suitable residence for the Governor, and which also provided office space for administration and public areas for official events. Old Government House is now within the grounds of the Queensland University of Technology and is a house museum.

ESSENTIAL SERVICES

Water

The first settlers drew water from the Brisbane River and other local waterways. As the town grew, the water from the river near the settlement became unsuitable for drinking and another water source was soon needed. The Enoggera Dam, built in 1866, was the first dam to supply Brisbane's water.

Most of the water for modern Brisbane relies on rain falling in the river catchments that feed the water reservoirs. The exception to this is the Gold Coast desalination plant that supplies drinking quality water to Brisbane and other nearby areas.

Many of the dams and reservoirs that store Brisbane's water allow public access for recreational activities such as boating and swimming, providing a large amount of open space for Greater Brisbane's people.

The Wivenhoe and Somerset Dams supply water to the Brisbane River and eventually to the Mount Crosby Weir and the taps of Brisbane. The dams also play a role in controlling floods through the managed release of water during times of heavy rain.

Electricity

The supply of electricity in Brisbane began in the 1880s. Today, Brisbane's electricity comes via the National Electricity Market, which pools resources and distributes power to five states and the ACT based on their needs.

Gas Supply

Brisbane had gas for street lighting and home use from the 1860s. The gas came from burning coal and it was distributed through gas pipes around the town. Today, Brisbane's consumers use natural gas which is a product of coal seam gas mining.

Lighting, Cooking and Heating in the Early 1800s

Before gas and electricity came along pipes and wires into houses, people used open fires for heating and cooking. Candles and oil lamps provided lighting.

The Wivenhoe Dam

BRISBANE'S PEOPLE

Jobs

People employed across Greater Brisbane work in a range of jobs in industries including building, health and welfare, technical services and retail.

Migration

Apart from those born in Australia, the next largest groups by country of birth in Greater Brisbane include people born in New Zealand, England, China, India and South Africa (2016 Census).

Density

Despite being the third largest city in Australia, Greater Brisbane has a low average population density per square kilometre. This contributes to its reputation as a city with a relaxed lifestyle. Within the city centre, the population density increases considerably. The population of Greater Brisbane will grow to about 3.3 million people by 2036.

'The Queenslander'

Housing

The Queenslander house is a style that is easily recognisable as belonging to the state. With wide verandas and built up high to cope with flooding from torrential rain, these timber houses are found throughout Brisbane's suburbs. Having an open lower floor area also allows air to circulate under the building, helping to keep it cool in the subtropical climate. The original Queenslander houses mostly date from the late 1800s and early 1900s.

TRANSPORT IN BRISBANE

Airports

In the 1920s, an airport operated at Eagle Farm in Brisbane. Situated at the mouth of the Brisbane River, Brisbane International Airport grew from these early beginnings.

Archerfield Airport is Brisbane's smaller airport, used now mainly by light aircraft and flying schools. The RAAF Base Amberley was a busy defence force base during the Second World War.

Trams

Horse-drawn trams operated in Brisbane from the 1880s. An electric tram service later took over from the horses. In 1969, Brisbane ceased running trams, and motor vehicles and buses became the main methods of road transport around the city.

Queen Street, Brisbane

Trains

The first trains in Queensland began running in 1865. Their main purpose was to carry freight from country areas to the port at Moreton Bay. From there, the freight loaded onto ships was carried to other locations in Australia or overseas. Unlike the other states, where most of the freight trains delivered their goods to a central port at the capital city, Queensland developed ports all along the coast. This enabled exporters further north to avoid having to send their freight all the way down to Brisbane when their purpose was to export it northward.

Brisbane's suburban trains went straight from being powered by steam to diesel power in the 1950s. Electrification of the city train services eventually began in the 1970s.

Brisbane River Transport

A ferry service in the early 1840s served the demands of the settlers for transport across the river before there were any bridges. Since then, ferries across the river have operated using rowboats, a paddle steamer, a punt and steam ferries.

Brisbane City Council operates a variety of water transport options on the Brisbane River:

CityCats – Catamarans named after Aboriginal place names along the Brisbane River

Ferries – Including the CityHopper Ferries offering transport for visitors to popular tourist points.

Larger, privately operated ferries serve the islands in Moreton Bay.

All the ferry wharves along the river were damaged in the 2011 floods, causing temporary suspension of services.

Victoria Bridge

The current Victoria Bridge is on the site of the first bridge across the Brisbane River. Built in 1865, this timber bridge soon began to rot and then collapsed in 1867. The current bridge was built in 1969.

INDUSTRY IN BRISBANE

Industries

Brisbane's main industries:

- Health care and social assistance
- Retail
- Professional, scientific and technical services
- Construction
- Education

Commercial Fishing

Fishing and aquaculture in Moreton Bay produce a large proportion of Brisbane's seafood, including prawns, crabs, oysters and fish.

Agriculture

Pasturing of animals is a major agricultural activity in Greater Brisbane, taking up over 30% of the entire land area. Farmers mostly raise poultry, graze cattle and grow strawberries, although there is also a wide range of other smaller operations producing all sorts of foods, garden products and timber from plantations.

Education

Providing high quality education to overseas students is a multi-billion dollar industry in Brisbane, with the Queensland University of Technology ranking well in international surveys.

TOURISM IN BRISBANE

Tourism is big business in Queensland and Brisbane. International advertising campaigns tempt tourists to visit the 'Sunshine State' and enjoy its sunny weather and beautiful locations.

The Ekka

The Royal Queensland Show is Brisbane's biggest annual event. It has been held since 1876 at the Brisbane Showgrounds. Known as the 'Ekka' (short for exhibition), the show attracts hundreds of thousands of people to enjoy the carnival atmosphere and look at agricultural displays and a variety of trade and other exhibitions.

Heart Reef in The Great Barrier Reef

Brisbane Ekka

Brisbane Ekka

Helping Visitors

Visitor Information Centres around Brisbane provide details on tours, accommodation and events and have maps to make a visit as stress-free as possible. Brisbane Greeters is a volunteer group that offers travellers to Brisbane a personal service to help them find their way around.

PLACES TO SEE IN BRISBANE

Bribie Island
Brisbane City Hall
Brisbane Lookout at Mt Coot-tha
Brisbane River
City Botanic Gardens
Commissariat Store
Eagle Street Pier
Fort Lytton National Park
Gallery of Modern Art
Kangaroo Point Cliffs
King George Square
Moreton Bay
Moreton Island

Gallery of Modern Art

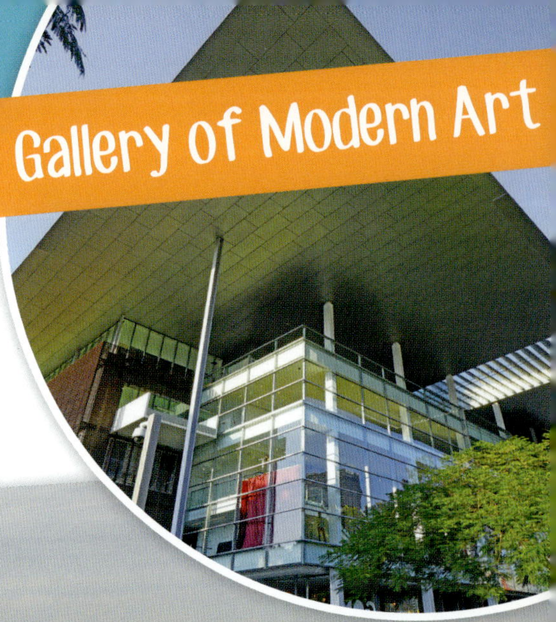

Mt Coot-tha Lookout

Brisbane Botanic Garden

Kangaroo Point Cliffs

Queen Street Mall

Newstead House
North Stradbroke Island
Old Government House
Old Windmill
Queen Street Mall
Queensland Art Gallery
Queensland Museum
Queensland Performing
Arts Centre
South Bank
St Helena Island ruins
Story Bridge (and its
Adventure Climb)
Wheel of Brisbane

North Stradbroke Island

Queensland Performing Arts Centre

SPORT IN BRISBANE

The Gabba, Brisbane Cricket Ground

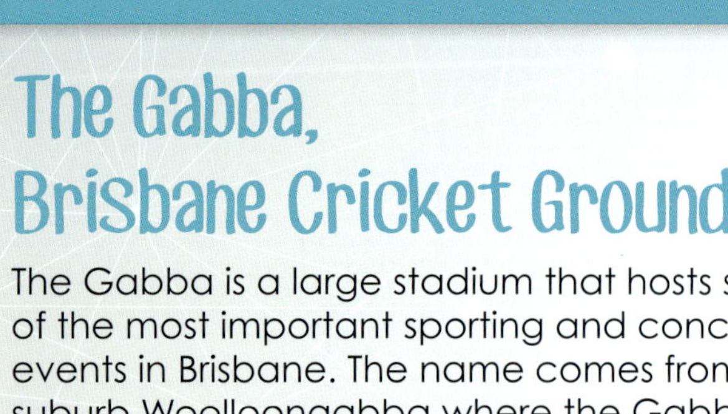

The Gabba is a large stadium that hosts some of the most important sporting and concert events in Brisbane. The name comes from the suburb Woolloongabba where the Gabba is located. Dating from the 1890s, a small area used for cricket gradually expanded to become this major city venue.

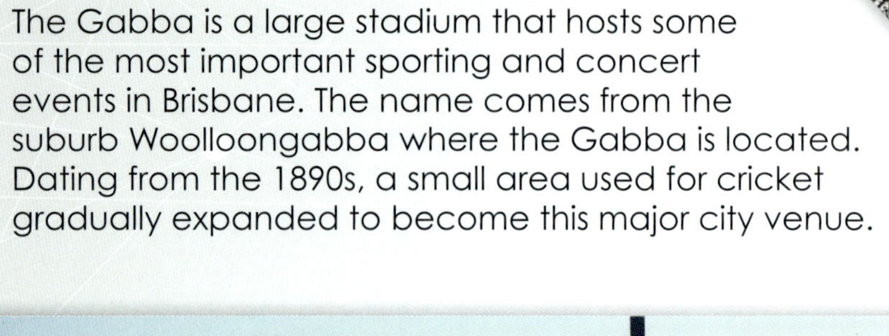

Commonwealth Games

The Commonwealth of Nations includes a third of the world's population, making it a continuing force in international affairs. The Commonwealth Games are held every four years.

2018

Brisbane was one of the event locations for the Gold Coast 2018 Commonwealth Games. The Shooting and Track Cycling events were held in Brisbane, just north of the Gold Coast, which was the official host city for the games.

1982

In 1982, Brisbane was the host city for the Commonwealth Games held that year.

GLOSSARY

aquifer natural underground water source
abundance large amount of something
aquaculture growing aquatic food creatures in enclosures
archaeology study of the remains of human history
breakwater structure built in the ocean to reduce the force of waves in the area
bunker defensive structure
catamaran boat with two hulls
commuter person who travels back and forth regularly for work
dialect variety within a language
dredge dig up a waterbed to make it deeper
era long period of time with special characteristics
idyllic peaceful and beautiful
ingest take into the mouth and swallow
inundate flood
jurisdiction legal right to have power in an area
midden ancient remains of rubbish
millennia thousands of years
millstone heavy stone used to grind grain into flour
quarantine keeping separate to stop disease spreading
silt-up fill a location with mud washed into it from the land
suffragettes women who fought for women's voting rights
temperate climate climate having mild temperatures – common in areas located just south of the Tropic of Capricorn, which runs through Rockhampton

INDEX

Settlement Cove Lagoon, Redcliffe, Brisbane

Bribie Island 16, 18
Brisbane City Council 8, 11, 20, 25
Brisbane City Hall 20
Brisbane River 4, 5, 8, 10, 13, 19, 22, 25
Bunya pines 7
cane toads 11
Commissariat Store 5, 9
Commonwealth Games 30
convicts 5, 8, 9, 19, 21
Ekka 27
electricity supply 8, 22, 24
emblems 20
Fisherman Island 15, 19
floods 10, 13, 22, 23, 25
Gabba 30
gas supply 22
Kangaroo Point 5, 28
King George Square 20
migration 23
Moreton Bay 4, 5, 6, 8, 9, 10, 14, 15-20, 24-26
Moreton Island 4, 5, 11, 16, 18,
native title 7
North Stradbroke Island 4, 7, 16, 18, 29
Old Government House 21
Old Windmill 5, 9
parliament 21
Petrie family 20
Quandamooka Nation 7
Second World War 18, 24
Streets Beach 17
Victoria Bridge 25
water supply 10, 13, 22, 20